# MY FIRST BOOK
# FIJI

## ALL ABOUT FIJI FOR KIDS

**GLOBED**
CHILDREN BOOKS

Copyright 2023 by Globed Children Books

All rights reserved. No part of this book may be reproduced or distributed in any form without prior written permission from the author, with the exception of non-commercial uses permitted by copyright law.

Limited of Liability/Disclaimer of Warranty: The publisher and author make no representations or liabilities with respect to the accuracy and completeness of the contents of this work and specifically disclaim all warranties including without limitations warranties of fitness of particular purpose. No warranty may be created or extended by sales or promotional materials. This work is sold with the understanding that the publisher and author is not engaging in rendering medical, legal or any other professional advice or service. Further, readers should be aware that websites listed in this work may have changed or disappeared between when this work was written and when it is read.

Interior and cover Design: Daniel Day
Editor: Margaret Bam

For My Sons, Daniel, David and Jude

*Matamanoa Island, Fiji*

# Fiji

Fiji is a **country**.

A country is land that is controlled by a **single government**. Countries are also called **nations, states, or nation-states**.

Countries can be **different sizes**. Some countries are big and others are small.

*Aerial view of Fiji Islands*

# Where Is Fiji?

Fiji is located in the continent of **Australia.**

A continent is **a massive area of land that is separated from others by water or other natural features**.

Fiji is situated in **Oceania**.

*Aerial view of Fiji Islands*

# Capital

The capital of Fiji is **Suva.**

Suva is located on the **south-eastern** Fiji.

Suva is the largest city in Fiji.

*Malolo Lailai Island, Fiji*

# Regions

Fiji is made up of fourteen provinces.

The provinces of Fiji are as follows:

**Ba, Bua, Cakaudrove, Kadavu, Lau, Lomaiviti, Macuata, Nadroga-Navosa, Naitasiri, Namosi, Ra, Rewa, Serua and Tailevu..**

*Malolo Lailai Island, Fiji*

# Population

Fiji has population of around **900,000 people** making it the 161st most populated country in the world and the 4th most populated country in **Oceania.**

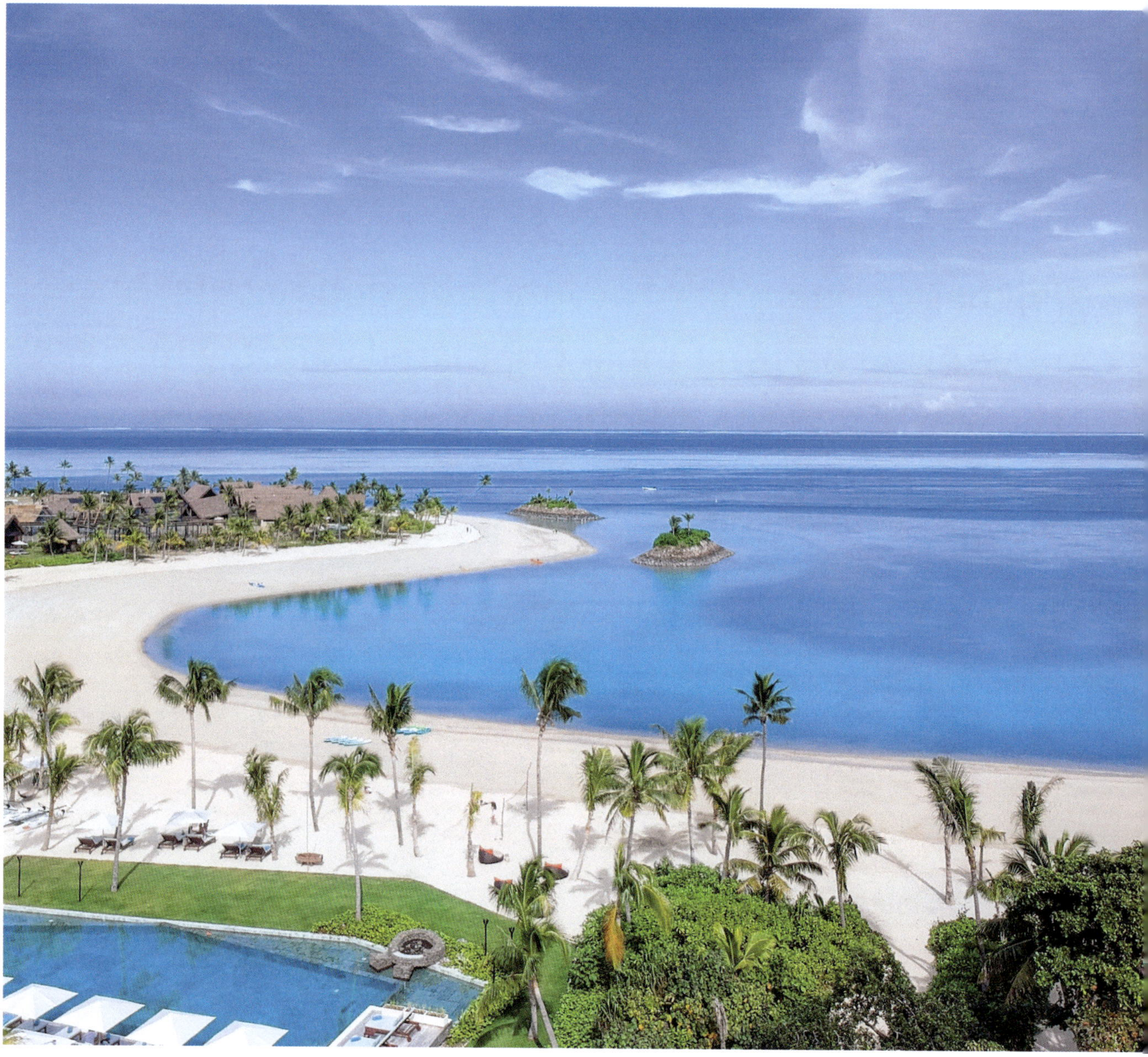

# Size

Fiji is **18,274 square kilometres** making it the 6th largest country in Oceania by area.

Fiji is the 151st largest country in the world.

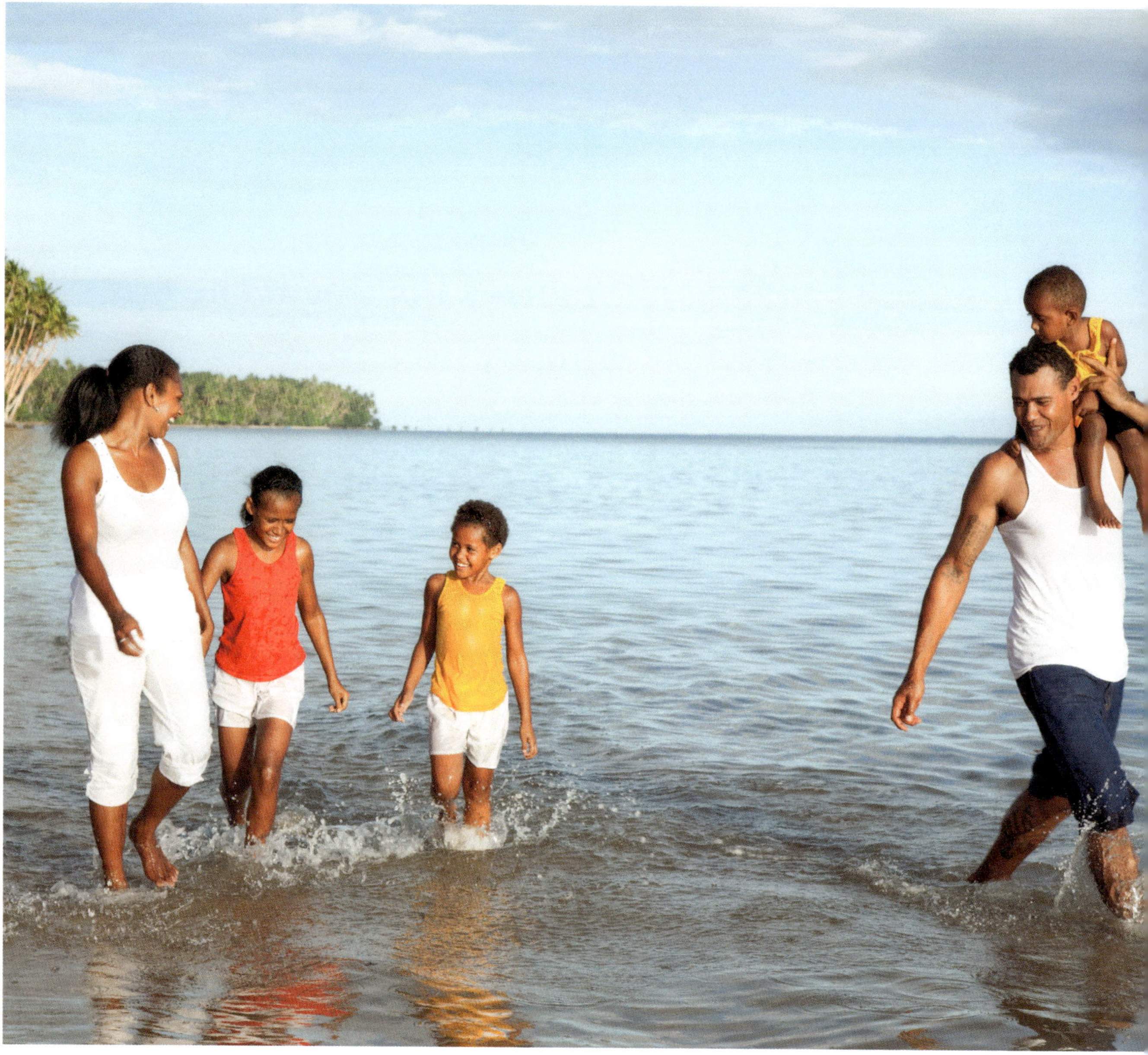

# Languages

The official language of Fiji is **Fijian, English and Fiji Hindi.**

The Fijian language originated in Fiji and is spoken by 350,000–450,000 ethnic Fijians as a native language.

Here are a few Fijian phrases
- **Sega na leqa** - No problem
- **Iko kai ve?** - Where are you from?
- **Bulabuka vinaka tiko** - How are you?

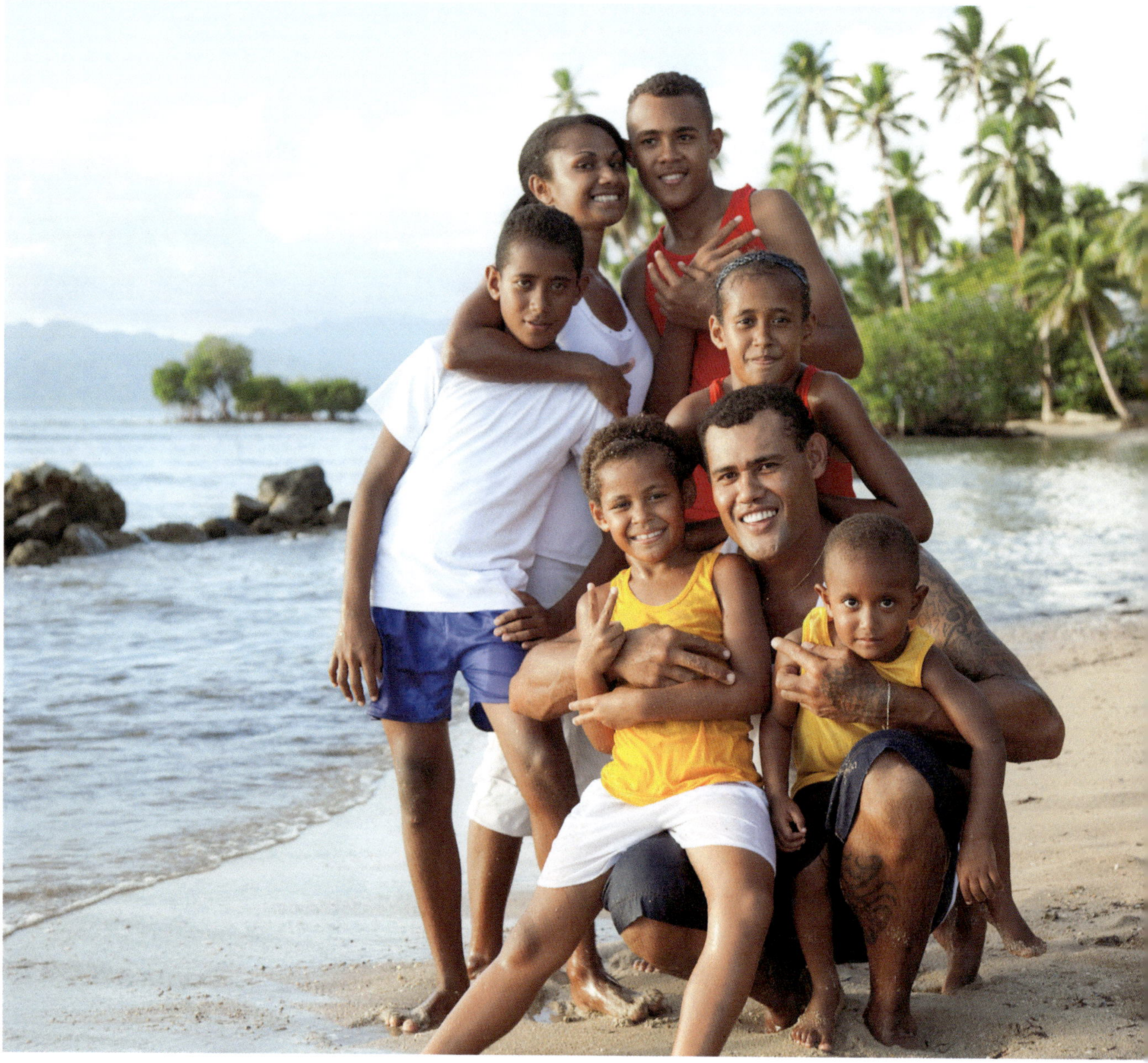

# Attractions

There are lots of interesting places to see in Fiji.

Some beautiful places to visit in Fiji are

- **Sri Siva Subramaniya Swami Temple**
- **Kula WILD Adventure Park**
- **Fiji Museum**
- **Garden of the Sleeping Giant**
- **Sigatoka Sand Dunes National Park**
- **Mamanuca Islands**

*Nadi, Fiji*

# History of Fiji

People have lived in Fiji for a very long time. In fact, it is believed that Fiji was settled by Austronesian peoples as far back as 3500 to 1000 BC.

In the 10th century, the Tu'i Tonga Empire was established in Tonga, and Fiji came within its sphere of influence. The Tongan influence brought Polynesian customs and language into Fiji.

**The British granted Fiji independence on October 10th 1970.**

*Fiji Heart Island*

# Customs in Fiji

Fiji has many fascinating customs and traditions.

- **Most Fijians have a strong belief in the family and community. It is not uncommon for buses to run a little late as the driver may stop to talk to friends or to help the family.**
- **It is considered as bad manners to touch a Fijian's head.**
- **Many Fijians are religious and believe in dressing modestly, the knees and shoulders are often covered when visiting relatives.**

*Suva, Fiji*

# Music of Fiji

There are many different music genres in Fiji such as **Bhajans, Qawaali and Dholak music.**

Some notable Fijian musicians include
- **Daniel Rae Costello**
- **George Veikoso**
- **Sakiusa Bulicokocoko**
- **Elena Baravilala**
- **Daren Kamali**
- **Mike Howlett**

*Kokoda, coconut milk ceviche*

# Food of Fiji

Fiji is known for its delicious, flavoursome and diverse food.

The national dish of Fiji is **Kokoda** which is a ceviche made using fish marinated in lime juice and served with a zingy salad.

*Fijian rice and dal dish*

# Food of Fiji

Some popular dishes in Fiji include

- **Lovo**
- **Kava**
- **Curry Chicken**
- **Lote**
- **Curry and Roti Parcel**
- **Freshly Baked Long Loaf with Rewa Butter**

*Vita Levu Island*

# Weather in Fiji

Fiji has a **tropical climate** with temperatures that remain relatively constant throughout the year, averaging around 23°C -25°C in the dry season (May-October) and 26°C -27°C in the wet season (November-April).

*Fiji Anemonefish*

# Animals of Fiji

There are many wonderful animals in Fiji.

Here are some animals that live in Fiji

- Dolphins
- Whales
- Sea turtles
- Eels
- Sea snakes

*Beach in Mamanuca Islands, Fiji*

# Beaches

There are many beautiful beaches in Fiji which is one of the reasons why so many people visit this beautiful country every year.

Here are some of Fiji's beaches

- **Natadola Beach**
- **Horseshoe Bay (Matangi Island)**
- **Malamala Island**
- **Castaway Island**
- **Beqa Island**

*Toberua Island, Fiji*

# Sports of Fiji

Sports play an integral part in Fijian culture. The most popular sport is **Rugby.**

Here are some of famous sportspeople from Fiji

- **Lote Tuqiri - Rugby**
- **Noa Nadruku - Rugby**
- **Waisale Serevi - Rugby**
- **Akapusi Qera - Rugby**

*Native Fijian statue - God of Fertility*

# Famous

Many successful people hail from Fiji.

Here are some notable Fijian figures

- Brij Vilash Lal – Historian
- Shamima Ali – Activist
- Imraz Iqbal Ali – Politician
- Jimmy Snuka – Wrestler
- Wilma Smith – Musician

*Snorkelers in Fiji*

# Something Extra...

As a little something extra, we are going to share some lesser known facts about Fiji.

- **Fiji is home to the largest temple in the Southern Hemisphere.**
- **Fiji is known as the soft coral capital of the world**

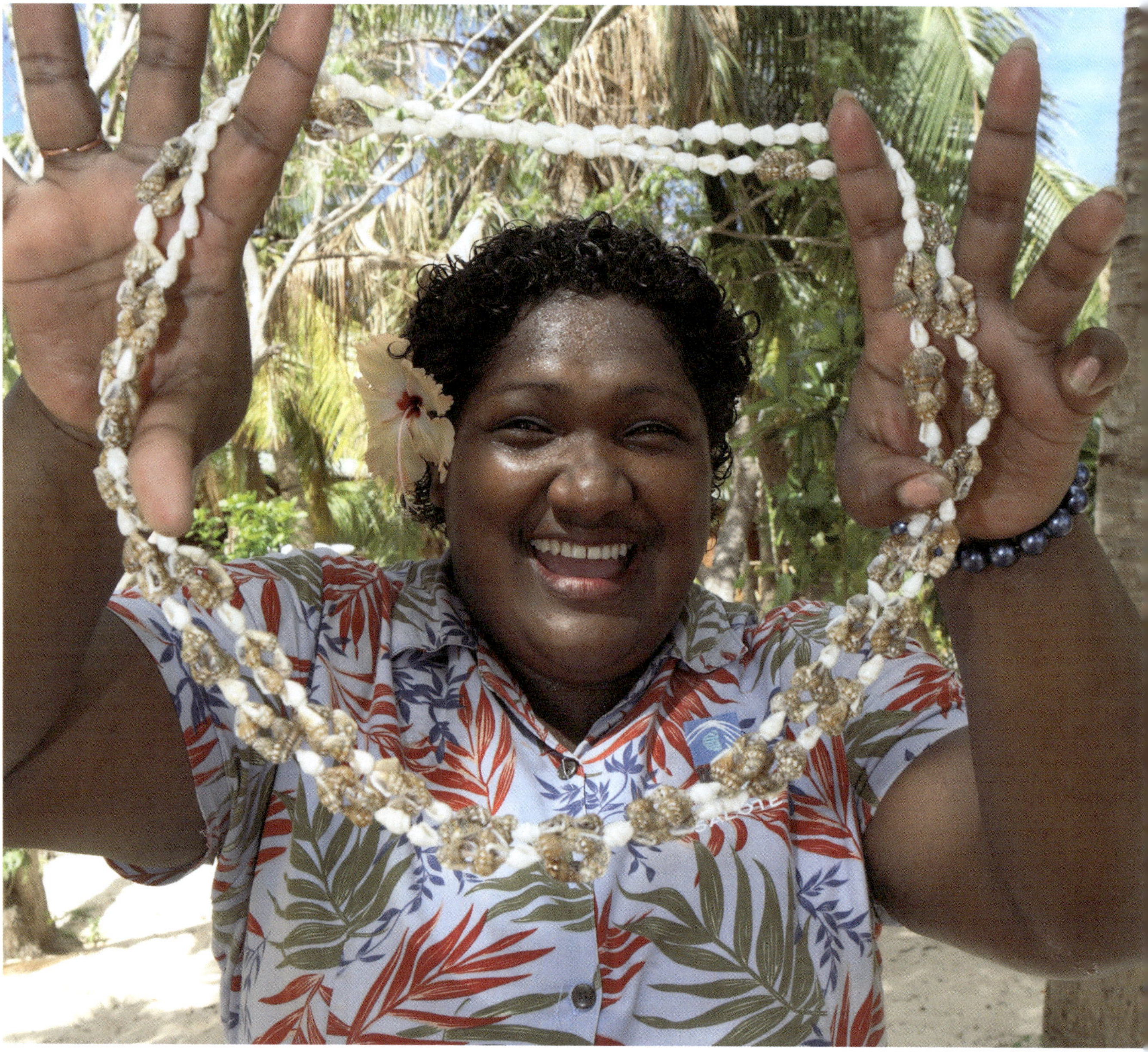

# Words From the Author

We hope that you enjoyed learning about the wonderful country of Fiji.

Fiji is a country rich in culture and beauty, with lots of wonderful places to visit and people to meet.

We hope you continue to learn more about this wonderful nation. If you enjoyed this book, consider leaving a review!

With Love

Printed in Great Britain
by Amazon